# The Old-... .... Trivia Book IV

## by Mel Simons

BearManor Media
2016

The Old-Time Radio Trivia Book IV

© 2016 Mel Simons

For information, address:

BearManor Media
P. O. Box 71426
Albany, GA  31708

bearmanormedia.com

Typesetting and layout by John Teehan

Published in the USA by BearManor Media

ISBN — 978-1-59393-962-5

# Dedication

This book is dedicated to Kenny Meyer. I was a regular for many years on two of Kenny's radio shows in Boston, *The Ken Meyer Show* on WBZ-AM and *Radio Classics* on WEEI-AM.

Kenny and I share the same love for old-time radio. We both listened as kids and still believe radio is the best medium.

Mel Simons
www.melsimons.net

*Marvin Kaplan*

# Foreword

I have never written a foreword for any book, and I'm probably the wrong person to do this, because I came in at the tail end of radio 1951-1955, and mostly performed in a comedy series, with only a few dramatic credits; but when Mel Simons, a true radio aficionado, approached me at the Sperdvac convention and asked me to write a foreword to his latest trivia book, I readily agreed.

My reasoning is simple: I love radio, I love performing in it, and I have a soft spot in my heart for all the topnotch pros whom I was fortunate enough to work with and know.

Hans Conried, one of the most taken-for-granted virtuosos and royalty amongst radio actors, had it right. He said he wished it was the other way around, that radio came after television. Few of us realized what a magnificent medium it was. Actors didn't have to memorize. Unless there was a studio audience, you didn't have to look or dress your best. You could still perform, even if you were in a wheelchair. The whole job lasted less than three hours. There was very little rehearsal. The cast usually gave topflight performances at the table read. But for that, you need experts who rarely or never fluffed, could fly without a net, and could do it in one take.

I have worked with a lot of people on these pages, either professionally or on the Local and National Boards of AFTRA. Bravo, Mel Simons, for being such a supporter and doing whatever you can to revive public interest in a magnificent medium, radio. As for you readers, exercising grey matter is a healthy pursuit and remember, nostalgia is not a disease.

*With kindest thoughts,*

– Marvin Kaplan
Radio: *Meet Millie*
Television: *Alice and Meet Millie*

*Mel Simons and Marvin Kaplan*

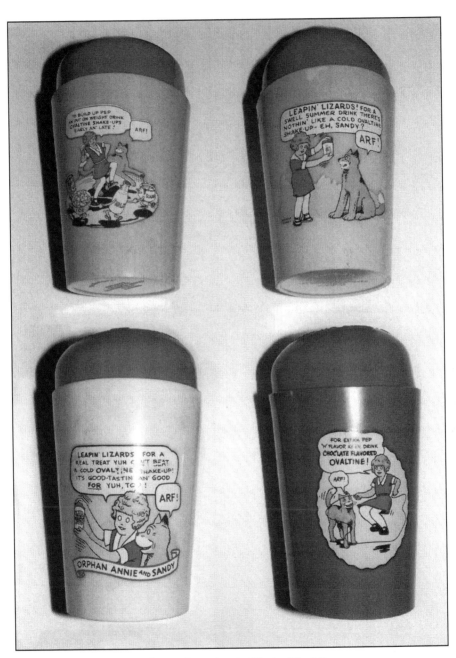

*Little Orphan Annie Shake-Up Mugs*

*Walter Tetley and Harold Peary – The Great Gildersleeve*

# Quiz #1

## THE GREAT GILDERSLEEVE

*(Answers on page 123)*

1. Where did Gildersleeve live?
2. What did he do for a living?
3. Name his long-time sponsor?
4. Who played Leroy?
5. What did Peavey do for a living?
6. Who played Birdie?
7. What was the name of Gildy's barber?
8. Who was Gildy's neighbor?
9. Who did Marjorie marry?
10. What was the name of Gildy's singing group?

*Jean Hersholt, Rosemary DeCamp* – Dr. Christian

# Quiz #2

## MATCH THE SPONSOR WITH THE SHOW

*(Answers on page 123)*

1. The Jack Benny Show
2. Straight Arrow
3. The Green Hornet
4. Dr. Christian
5. Suspense
6. Amos 'n' Andy
7. The Falcon
8. Tom Mix
9. Gangbusters
10. The Whistler


a. Ralston
b. Rinso
c. Jello
d. Vaseline
e. Nabisco
f. Signal Oil
g. Gem Blades
h. Orange Crush
i. Autolite
j. Waterman's Pens

*Vincent Price*

# Quiz #3

**VINCENT PRICE**
*(Answers on Page 124)*

1. Vincent went to which Ivy League college?

2. His first job on radio was on which soap opera?

3. On the radio show *Escape*, what was his most famous episode?

4. Name the radio show he is best known for.

5. What was his character's name on that show?

6. What was his profession on the show?

7. He is one of the world's biggest collectors of what?

8. Name the early 3-D movie he appeared in.

9. On the *Sears Radio Theater*, he hosted which Wednesday night format?

10. On PBS Television, he hosted what?

*Peg Lynch and Alan Bunce* – Ethel and Albert

*Raymond Edward Johnson* – Inner Sanctum

*Dean Martin and Jerry Lewis*

# Quiz #4

**RELATIONSHIPS (match the relationship)**

*(Answers on Page 124)*

1. Judy and Dr. Christian
2. Ida and Eddie
3. Bud and Lou
4. Oogie and Judy
5. Reggie and Archie
6. Mary and Henry
7. Chester and Matt
8. Henry and Sunday
9. Perry and Clark
10. George and Groucho

 

a. Announcer
b. Nurse
c. Sister
d. Wife
e. Editor
f. Husband
g. Boyfriend
h. Partner
i. Rival
j. Deputy

*Nigel Bruce and Basil Rathbone* – Sherlock Holmes

# Quiz #5

## COMMERCIALS

*(Answers on Page 124)*

1. The incredible, edible _____.

2. _____ keeps your car on the go.

3. Bet you can't eat just one. _____ Potato Chips.

4. _____, the skin you love to touch.

5. In the valley of the jolly _____ _____.

6. _____ _____ helps build strong bodies twelve ways.

7. Kellogg's _____, the super delicious cereal.

8. Trust the _____ Fisherman.

9. I could have had a _____.

10. This _____ for you.

*Tommy Dorsey*

*Don Ameche*

# Quiz #6

## WHO SAID?
*(Answers on Page 125)*

1.  "Well, now, I wouldn't say that."
2.  "You're a hard man, McGee."
3.  "You betchum, Red Ryder."
4.  "Plunk your magic twanger, Froggie."
5.  "Evenin', folks. How y'all?"
6.  "Stop da music!"
7.  "Who's Yehudi?"
8.  "Thanks for listening."
9.  "Whatcha' doin' mistah? Huh? Whatcha' doin'?"
10. "Nobody's home. I hope, I hope, I hope."

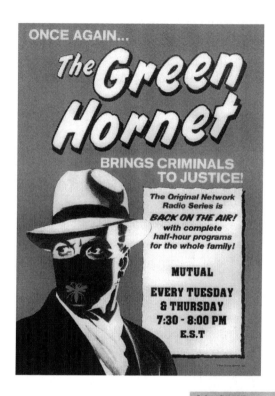

*Lauren Bacall and Humphrey Bogart* – Bold Venture

*Ozzie and Harriet*

# Quiz #7

## OZZIE & HARRIET
*(Answers on Page 125)*

1.  What are their last names?

2.  They got their start on radio on whose show?

3.  What did Ozzie do for a living?

4.  Name their long-time orchestra leader.

5.  Who was their sponsor?

6.  Janet Waldo played what character on the show?

7.  They had the same announcer for years. Who was it?

8.  Who was their next-door neighbor?

9.  What was their home address?

10. Harriet began her career as a singer for whose orchestra?

*Eddie 'Rochester' Anderson* – The Jack Benny Show

*Lon Clark* – Nick Carter, Master Detective

*Radio ads*

*Goodman and Jane Ace* – Easy Aces

*Virginia Payne* – Ma Perkins

# Quiz #8

## MATCH THE SAYING WITH THE RADIO PERSONALITY

*(Answers on Page 125)*

1. "Everybody's gotta get into di act."
2. "The weed of crime bears bitter fruit."
3. "Good night, Nicky darling."
4. "Love dat man."
5. "Nice."
6. "Friends, and you are my friends."
7. "Hello nephews, nieces, mine."
8. "Ooooh, what's gonna happen to him?"
9. "Mr. Autery."
10. "Don't ever do that."


a. Ralph Edwards
b. Jimmy Durante
c. Uncle Don
d. The Shadow
e. Joe Penner
f. Pat Buttram
g. Nora Charles
h. Midnight, the cat
i. Beulah
j. Ersel Twing

*Al Jolson*

*Chico and Groucho Marx*

*Arnold Stang*

# Quiz #9

## ARNOLD STANG
*(Answers on Page 126)*

1. Arnold's first job on radio was on which children's program?

2. Name his most famous children's show.

3. He appeared on *The Goldbergs* for nine years. Which character did he play?

4. On that show who did he have a crush on?

5. Name the character he played on *The Milton Berle Television Show*.

6. Arnold is best remembered for what radio show?

7. What character did he play on that show?

8. What was his name on *The Milton Berle Television Show*?

9. Name the movie he did with Frank Sinatra.

10. He was the voice of which cartoon character?

*The Andrews Sisters*

# Quiz #10

## THE ANDREW SISTERS
*(Answers on Page 126)*

1. Name the three Andrews sisters.

2. What was their hometown?

3. Name the bandleader who was their co-star on *The Chesterfield Radio Show*.

4. Name their first hit record.

5. What was their biggest-selling record?

6. Name the comedian who wrote that song.

7. The sisters have the biggest-selling polka record in history. Name the polka.

8. What were the two hit records they had with the word apple?

9. After she retired from singing, which sister taught speech and drama in college?

10. Name the Broadway show based on their lives.

*Big Little Books*

# Quiz #11

**HOME TOWNS (Match the home town with the radio star)**

*(Answers on Page 126)*

1. Fred Allen
2. Bing Crosby
3. Rudy Vallee
4. Jean Hersholt
5. Frank Sinatra
6. Kay Kyser
7. Dinah Shore
8. Perry Como
9. Al Jolson
10. Walter Winchell


a. Hoboken, New Jery
b. New York, New York
c. Somerville, Massachusetts
d. Petersburg, Russia
e. Winchester, Tennessee
f. Tacoma, Washington
g. Rocky Mount, North Carolina
h. Copenhagen, Denmark
i. Westbrook, Maine
j. Cannonsburgh, Pennsylvania

*Ken Roberts*

# Quiz #12

## GENERAL QUESTIONS
*(Answers on Page 127)*

1. Who was Yukon King?

2. Randy Stone was a reporter for which newspaper?

3. Who was the leader of the City Slickers?

4. Name the character that Harry Einstein played.

5. Who operated the telegraph machine on *The Walter Winchell Radio Show*?

6. Ozzie and Harriet got their start on whose radio show?

7. Who played Rochester?

8. Name Hedda Hopper's number one rival.

9. What was Captain Midnight's real name?

10. Herb Morrison announced what famous disaster?

*Claire Trevor, Edward G. Robinson* – Big Town

# Quiz #13

## TRUE OR FALSE
*(Answers on Page 127)*

1. William Spier directed *Suspense*.

2. *Juvenile Jury* was hosted by Bud Collyer.

3. *Bulldog Drummond* began with footsteps and a fog horn.

4. Irene Wicker was "The Singing Lady."

5. Theresa Brewer sang on *Your Hit Parade*.

6. Tom Howard was the quizmaster on *Can You Top This?*

7. Judy Canova played herself on *The Judy Canova Show*.

8. The bandleader on *So You Want to Lead a Band* was Kay Kyser.

9. Jackson Beck played the "Cisco Kid."

10. Ezra Stone of *The Aldrich Family* directed the show when it came to television.

# Quiz #14

## GENERAL QUESTIONS
*(Answers on Page 127)*

1.  Who played Dr. Christian?

2.  Name the bandleader who was known as "The King of Jazz."

3.  Joan Davis starred in which radio show?

4.  Who was the man with the action-packed expense account?

5.  Name the program that began with footsteps, a foghorn and two gun shots.

6.  What does LSMFT stand for?

7.  Who sponsored Milton Berle on radio?

8.  Name the Ameche brothers.

9.  Who played Singing Sam?

10. Name the detective that Jack Webb played before *Dragnet*.

# Quiz #15

## MATCH THE SAYING WITH THE RADIO PERSONALITY

*(Answers on Page 128)*

1. "Coming, mother."
2. "Who is buried in Grant's Tomb?"
3. "How are ya, how are ya, how are ya?"
4. "Good day."
5. "Write if you get work, and hang by your thumbs."
6. "We remain yours for bigger and better laughs."
7. "Well, Daisy June…"
8. "Holy mackerel, Andy."
9. "Your loving son…"
10. "McGeeeeee."

a. Bob and Ray
b. Paul Harvey
c. Henry Aldrich
d. Mayor LaTrivia
e. George "Kingfish" Stevens
f. Ward Wilson
g. Groucho Marx
h. Arthur Godfrey
i. Clem Kadiddlehopper
j. Luigi Basco

*Elliott Lewis*

# Quiz #16

## MATCH THE BANDLEADER WITH HIS VOCALIST

*(Answers on Page 128)*

1. Bing Crosby
2. Rosemary Clooney
3. Ella Fitzgerald
4. Mel Torme
5. Bea Wain
6. Al Hibbler
7. Martha Tilton
8. Perry Como
9. Marion Hutton
10. Mildred Bailey

 

a. Benny Goodman
b. Duke Ellington
c. Larry Clinton
d. Paul Whiteman
e. Glenn Miller
f. Chico Marx
g. Tony Pastor
h. Chick Webb
i. Red Norvo
j. Ted Weems

*Ed Gardner* – Duffy's Tavern

# Quiz #17

## FIRST AND LAST NAMES
*(Answers on Page 128)*

1. *The Great Gildersleeve*
   Judge Hooker's first name

2. *Amos 'n' Andy*
   Amos' last name

3. *Duffy's Tavern*
   Finnegan's first name

4. *Just Plain Bill*
   Bill's last name

5. *Fred Allen Show*
   Mrs. Nussbaum's first name

6. *Archie Andrews*
   Judhead's last name

7. *Our Miss Brooks*
   Mr. Conklin's first name

8. *The Shadow*
   Lamont's last name

9. *Dr. Christian*
   Dr. Christian's first name

10. *Blondie*
    Dagwood's last name

*Jack Benny, Danny Kaye, Dinah Shore*

# Quiz #18

## GENERAL QUESTIONS
*(Answers on Page 129)*

1. Name the cereal that was "crispy and crunchy the whole year through."

2. Where did the "elite meet to eat"?

3. What was the name of Bulldog Drummond's assistant?

4. Who was Richard Kollmar, radio's Boston Blackie, married to?

5. Name the lady that played the magic violin.

6. Who co-starred with Fanny Brice on *Maxwell House Coffee Time*?

7. Mae West often guested on which radio show?

8. Who was known as "The Vagabond Lover"?

9. Name the show that had a laugh meter.

10. Rosa was the girlfriend of whom?

*William Conrad* – Gunsmoke

# Quiz #19

## TRUE OR FALSE
*(Answers on Page 129)*

1. Jack Benny made his radio debut on Ed Sullivan's radio show.

2. "The Mysterious Traveler" always said, "I know many things for I walk by night."

3. Nick Carter was known as "The Armchair Detective."

4. Weddings were often performed on *Bride and Groom*.

5. Richard Widmark was the first Albert on *Ethel and Albert*.

6. Sportscaster Red Barber's favorite catch phrase was "How about that?"

7. Rose Marie was a child star on radio.

8. Joe Penner was radio's "Baron Munchhausen."

9. The character Miss Spaulding appeared on *Life With Luigi*.

10. Arnold Stang once had his own radio show.

*Mary Livingston – Dennis Day*

# Quiz #20

## DENNIS DAY
*(Answers on Page 129)*

1.  What is Dennis' real name?

2.  What year did he start on *The Jack Benny Show*?

3.  Name the singer that he replaced.

4.  Who played his mother on Jack's show?

5.  What was the name of his own radio show?

6.  What type of work did he do on his show?

7.  Name his girlfriend on the show.

8.  Name the character he played in an animated movie.

9.  Name his famous Irish novelty song.

10. Dennis had one top-ten song. What was it?

*Mini Comic Books*

# Quiz #21

## MULTIPLE CHOICE
*(Answers on Page 130)*

1.  Who was not a sponsor of the *Phil Harris-Alice Faye Show?*
    a) Fitch  b) Dentine  c) Rexall

2.  What instrument did Glenn Miller play?
    a) trumpet  b) saxophone  c) trombone

3.  Name the mystery show that opened with a squeaking door.
    a) *Inner Sanctum*  b) *Suspense*  c) *The Haunting Hour*

4.  The A-1 Detective Agency was featured on what show?
    a) *The House of Mystery*  b) *The Detectives*
    c) *I Love a Mystery*

5.  Edward Arnold was the star of which show?
    a) *The Great Gatsby*  b) *Mr. President*
    c) *Grand Central Station*

6.  Ivan Shark was an arch enemy of which Captain?
    a) Captain Marvel  b) Captain Midnight
    c) Captain Kangaroo

7.  The show *Twenty Questions* was sponsored by –
    a) Ronson  b) Gillette  c) Ipana

8.  Which comedian was known as "The Fire Chief?"
    a) Fred Allen  b) Milton Berle  c) Ed Wynn

9.  Who played "The Magic Violin"?
    a) Evelyn  b) Marjorie  c) Joanne

10. Name the singer on *The Chesterfield Supper Club.*
    a) Midy Carson  b) Doris Day  c) Jo Stafford

*Brace Beemer – The Lone Ranger*

*Tom Mix*

*Henry Morgan – Here's Morgan*

# Quiz #22

## COMEDIANS
*(Answers on Page 130)*

1. Phil Silvers
2. Bob Hope
3. Judy Canova
4. Ozzie and Harriet
5. Garry Moore
6. Bob Burns
7. Johnny Carson
8. Joey Bishop
9. Vic and Sade
10. Red Skelton
11. Goodman Ace
12. Larry David
13. Amos 'n' Andy
14. Lou Lehr
15. Jerry Seinfeld

*Ronald Colman and Benita Hume* – The Halls of Ivy

*Penny Singleton and Arthur Lake* – Blondie

*Clayton 'Bud' Collyer* – Superman

*Fibber McGee and Molly*

# Quiz #23

## FIBBER McGEE AND MOLLY
*(Answers on Page 131)*

1. Name the long-time orchestra leader.

2. Who said, "Hi ya, Johnny?"

3. Mayor La Trivia was played by whom?

4. What was the name of the McGees' maid?

5. Who was the henpecked husband?

6. Name the telephone operator.

7. When Fibber said something that he thought was funny, what would Molly always say?

8. Who were Don Quinn and Phil Leslie?

9. The show was on every Tuesday night. What time was it on?

10. What did Molly say at the end of the show?

*Shirley Mitchell* – The Great Gildersleeve

*Perry Como, Jo Stafford, Arthur Godfrey*

*Jack Benny, Phil Silvers*

# Quiz #24

**JACK BENNY**
*(Answers on Page 131)*

1.  What was Jack's real name?

2.  Where did he grow up?

3.  Who was his closest friend?

4.  Name his first male singer.

5.  What branch of the service was Jack in?

6.  Who played the floor walker?

7.  Who played Dennis' mother?

8.  What did Phil Harris call Mary?

9.  Who said, "Psst, hey bud. C'mere a minute."

10. What was the name of Jack's violin teacher?

*Fred Allen*

# Quiz #25

**FRED ALLEN**

*(Answers on Page 131)*

1. Name the alley that Fred would visit each week.

2. What was Mrs. Nussbaum's first name?

3. What was her husband's first name?

4. How many DeMarco Sisters were there?

5. Name Fred's first show on radio.

6. Fred often played a Chinese detective. What was his name?

7. What was Senator Claghorn's first name?

8. He was played by whom?

9. Name the famous author who was once a writer for Fred's show.

10. What did Fred often say about Old Orchard?

*Frank Lovejoy* – Nightbeat

*Albert Aley* – Hope Harrigan

*Alan Ladd* – Box 13

*Tom Howard and George Shelton* – It Pays To Be Ignorant

# Quiz #26

## COMMERCIALS

*(Answers on Page 132)*

1. Keep cookin' with _____.

2. Thirty-three fine beers, blended into one great beer _____ _____ beer.

3. Better buy _____.

4. Ask any mermaid you happen to see, "What's the best tuna?" _____ ___ ___ _____.

5. All the world is serene, in that moment supreme, when you're smoking a _____ cigar.

6. You can be sure if it's _____.

7. If it's not your mother, it's _____ _____.

8. If you wash with _____ _____ tonight, tomorrow your hair will be sunshine bright.

9. _____ kills bugs dead.

10. There's something about an _____ _____ man.

*The panel members of* Can You Top This? *(left to right) Peter Donald,* *"Senator" Ed Ford, Ward Wilson, Harry Hershfield*

# Quiz #27

## MULTIPLE CHOICE
*(Answers on Page 132)*

1. What did Chester Riley call his son?
   a) Butch b) Junior c) Kid

2. Who created *The CBS Mystery Theater*?
   a) Himan Brown b) Ezra Stone c) Ralph Bell

3. Name the Kay who sang on *Stop the Music*.
   a) Kay Starr b) Kay Armen c) Kay Kyser

4. When Penny Singleton left *Blondie*, who replaced her?
   a) Betty Hutton b) Ann Rutherford c) Betty White

5. What subject did Mr. Boynton teach on *Our Miss Brooks*?
   a) Chemistry b) Algebra c) Biology

6. Name the editor of *The Illustrated Press*.
   a) Steve Wilson b) Perry White c) Randy Stone

7. Who sang on *The Jack Benny Show*?
   a) Frank Parker b) Kenny Baker c) Dennis Day

8. Name the bandleader who was known for his "Rippling Rhythm."
   a) Bob Crosby b) Stan Kenton c) Shep Fields

9. Who was known as "The Street Singer"?
   a) Phil Harris b) Art Lund c) Arthur Tracy

10. Name the wife of Lorenzo Jones.
    a) Belle b) Janet c) Ruth

*Harry James*

# Quiz #28

## SOAP OPERAS
*(Answers on Page 132)*

1. Who wrote *One Man's Family*?

2. Mary Jane Higby was the star of which soap?

3. The song "Rose of Tralee" was the theme for which show?

4. Who was the girl intern?

5. How were Myrt and Marge related?

6. What was the name of Stella Dallas' daughter?

7. Who was Ellen Brown?

8. What year did soap operas begin on radio?

9. Who told *True Life Stories*?

10. What did Ma Perkins do for a living?

*James Stewart* – The Six Shooter

# Quiz #29

## GENERAL QUESTIONS
*(Answers on Page 133)*

1. Who was America's "Ace of the Airwaves"?

2. Name the crime-fighting show that began with sirens and guns.

3. Who was the producer-director of *House Party*?

4. Who was the first Lone Ranger?

5. The routine "Who's on First?" was performed by whom?

6. Who played the first Riley in *The Life of Riley*?

7. Name the show that was "The Crossroads of a Million Public Lives."

8. Who ended her show saying, "Thanks for listening. Good night, folks."?

9. Which show began with "It... is... later... than... you... think"?

10. What did Little Jack Little do?

Tony Martin
Tony Martin Time

Bill Stern
Sportscaster

Olan Soule & Barbara Luddy
The First Nighter

Eli Mintz
Uncle David in The Goldbergs

*Gum cards*

# Quiz #30

## DRAGNET
*(Answers on Page 133)*

1.  What was Jack Webb's name on the show?
2.  What was his rank with the police department?
3.  Name the police department.
4.  Who did he live with?
5.  Name his first partner.
6.  Name his second partner.
7.  What was his badge number?
8.  Why was that his number?
9.  What was his most famous saying?
10. Who wrote the *Dragnet* theme?

*Dennis Day and Don Wilson*

# Quiz #31

## FILL IN THE SHOW
*(Answers on Page 133)*

1. This is your host, welcoming you into the
   _____ _____.

2. Look, up in the air. It's a bird, it's a plane, it's
   _____.

3. Enemy to those who make him an enemy. Friend
   to those who have no friends. _____
   _____.

4. A tale well calculated to keep you in
   _____.

5. _____ _____ _____ ... Champion of the
   People.

6. And now, smile a while with _____
   _____ and his wife Belle.

7. From out of the past come the thundering hoof-
   beats of the great horse Silver. ____ _____
   _____ rides again.

8. And now, Oxydol's own _____
   _____.

9. Out of the fog... out of the night... and into
   his American adventure... comes _____
   _____.

10. Period. End of report. _____ _____.

*Radio ads*

# Quiz #32

## MATCH THE SAYING WITH THE RADIO PERSONALITY

*(Answers on Page 134)*

1. "You're looking fine, Riley. Very natural."
2. "Look out, Jerry. He's got a gun."
3. "Isn't that awful?"
4. "Good night to you, and you, and I do mean you."
5. "You're a hard man, McGee."
6. "I hope, I hope, I hope."
7. "This is my dog, Tige, and he lives in there, too."
8. "Here he is, the only and only, Groucho."
9. "I'll run your little finger through the pencil sharpener."
10. "Well, Portland, gee whiz."

 

a. Buster Brown
b. The Great Gildersleeve
c. Jimmy Fidler
d. Mr. Dithers
e. Digger O'Dell
f. Fred Allen
g. Pamela North
h. Goodman Ace
i. Al Pearce
j. George Fenneman

*Alice Faye* – Phil Harris/Alice Faye Show

*William Bendix* – The Life of Riley

*Gene Autry*

# Quiz #33

## GENE AUTRY
*(Answers on Page 134)*

1. What was the name of Gene's radio show?

2. Name his long-time sponsor.

3. What was the name of his sidekick?

4. What did the sidekick always call Gene?

5. Name Gene's vocal group.

6. What was Gene's theme song?

7. Who was Gene's announcer?

8. How did the announcer introduce Gene?

9. What was Gene's biggest-selling record?

10. Name the baseball team that Gene owned.

*Frankie Laine – The Big Show*

*Freeman Gosden and Charles Correll* – Amos 'n' Andy

# Quiz #34

## MULTIPLE CHOICE
*(Answers on Page 134)*

1.  Radio was introduced in automobiles in what year?
    a)   1929   b)  1931   c)  1934

2.  Who went to Hudson High School?
    a)   Archie Andrews   b)  Jack Armstrong   c)  Henry Aldrich

3.  Sam Spade's secretary was whom?
    a)   Amy   b)  Effie   c)  Marsha

4.  Lauren Becall co-starred on which radio show?
    a)   House of Mystery   b)  Escape   c)  Bold Venture

5.  Name the toothpaste that sponsored The Mel Blanc Show.
    a)   Pepsodent   b)  Colgate   c)  Ipana

6.  Who appeared the most times on Suspense?
    a)   Bette Davis   b)  Cathy Lewis   c)  Agnes Moorehead

7.  Tallulah Bankhead hosted which radio show?
    a)   The Big Broadcast   b)  Escape   c)  Showboat

8.  Name the sheriff on The Tom Mix Show.
    a)   Mike Shaw   b)  Billy Batson   c)  Ralph Bell

9.  Who was an animal trainer?
    a)   Billy Batson   b)  Jack Mather   c)  Clyde Beatty

10. Name the emcee of Life Begins at 80.
    a)   Jack Hines   b)  Jack Barry   c)  Jack London

*Martha Tilton*

# Quiz #35

## MATCH THE RADIO STAR WITH THE MOVIE
*(Answers on Page 135)*

1. Dean Martin
2. Milton Berle
3. Roy Rogers
4. Basil Rathbone
5. Glenn Miller
6. Abbott and Costello
7. Edward G. Robinson
8. Mario Lanza
9. Mickey Rooney
10. Arthur Godfrey


a. *Buck Privates*
b. *The Great Caruso*
c. *Always Leave Them Laughing*
d. *The Glass Bottom Boat*
e. *The Sons of Katie Elder*
f. *Strike Up The Band*
g. *Son of Paleface*
h. *Orchestra Wives*
i. *The Hound of the Baskervilles*
j. *Double Indemnity*

*Red Skelton*

# Quiz #36

## RED SKELTON
*(Answers on Page 135)*

1. What is Red's real first name?

2. Who was Red's longtime band leader?

3. What was the name of the "Mean Widdle Kid"?

4. What was the kid's most famous line?

5. Red's character, Willie Lump-Lump, was known as what?

6. What was Willie's most famous routine?

7. Name Red's theme song?

8. Red's punch-drunk boxer was whom?

9. Name Red's vocal group.

10. What was Clem Kadiddlehopper's opening line?

*Marie Wilson* – My Friend Irma

# Quiz #37

## MATCH THE DETECTIVE SHOW WITH THE ACTOR

*(Answers on Page 135)*

1. Howard Duff
2. Dick Powell
3. Vincent Price
4. Lon Clark
5. J. Scott Smart
6. Jack Webb
7. Statts Cotsworth
8. Richard Kollmar
9. Jackson Beck
10. Jeff Chandler


a. *The Saint*
b. *Nick Carter*
c. *Sam Spade*
d. *Michael Shayne*
e. *Philo Vance*
f. *Richard Diamond*
g. *The Fat Man*
h. *Dragnet*
i. *Casey, Crime Photographer*
j. *Boston Blackie*

*Fanny Brice – Baby Snooks*

# Quiz #38

## FANNY BRICE
*(Answers on Page 136)*

1. What was her real name?

2. Name the Broadway show in which she introduced Baby Snooks.

3. Who was her closest friend in that show?

4. What was her biggest-selling record?

5. Name her three husbands.

6. How old was Baby Snooks?

7. Where did Snooks live?

8. Name the radio show she shared with Frank Morgan.

9. Name the two movies based on her life.

10. Who played Fanny in both movies?

*Edgar Bergen and Charlie McCarthy*

# Quiz #39

## EDGAR BERGEN – CHARLIE McCARTHY
*(Answers on Page 136)*

1. What did Charlie wear over his right eye?

2. Edgar had one female dummy. What was her name?

3. Charlie had a feud with which famous comedian?

4. Pat Patrick played which character on the show?

5. What was the character's opening remark?

6. What did Edgar always say to Mortimer Snerd?

7. Name Charlie's most famous saying?

8. The Bickersons got their start on this show. What were their first names?

9. Name their long-time orchestra leader.

10. Name their two sponsors.

*Roy Rogers and Dale Evans*

*The Sportsmen Quartet* – The Jack Benny Show

*Fred Allen and Jimmy Durante*

*Harlow Wilcox*

*Fred Allen*

# Quiz #40

## CIGARETTE COMMERCIALS
## (Fill in the cigarette.)
*(Answers on Page 136)*

1. I'd walk a mile for a _____.

2. Willie, the Penguin says, "Smoke _____."

3. Call for _____ _____.

4. _____ tastes good, like a cigarette should.

5. To a smoker, it's a _____.

6. This is it, _____ _____ _____ filters.

7. _____ _____ cigarettes, outstanding, and they are mild.

8. You can take _____ out of the country, but you can't take the country out of _____.

9. _____ filter cigarettes.

10. _____ _____ mean fine tobacco.

# Quiz #41

## MATCH THE TOWN WITH THE SHOW
*(Answers on Page 137)*

1. Wistful Vista
2. Dodge
3. Pine Ridge
4. Madison
5. Silver Creek
6. Summerfield
7. Rushville Center
8. Riverdale
9. Centerville
10. Hartville

a. *The Great Gildersleeve*
b. *Archie Andrews*
c. *Just Plain Bill*
d. *Gunsmoke*
e. *Fibber McGee & Molly*
f. *Our Gal Sunday*
g. *The Aldrich Family*
h. *Lum 'n' Abner*
i. *Ma Perkins*
j. *Our Miss Brooks*

# Quiz #42

## MATCH THE QUIZ SHOW WITH ITS HOST

*(Answers on Page 137)*

1. *What's My Line?*
2. *Information Please*
3. *College Quiz Bowl*
4. *Double or Nothing*
5. *Doctor I.Q.*
6. *Down You Go*
7. *Quick As a Flash*
8. *Stop the Music*
9. *Beat the Band*
10. *Strike It Rich*

a. Bert Parks
b. Warren Hull
c. Clifton Fadiman
d. John Daley
e. Win Elliot
f. Allen Ludden
g. Walter O'Keefe
h. Bergen Evans
i. Lew Valentine
j. Marvin Miller

*Radio ads*

# Quiz #43

## RELATIONSHIPS (March the relationship.)

*(Answers on Page 137)*

1.  Irma and Jane
2.  Babs and Junior
3.  Effie and Sam
4.  Pam and Jerry
5.  David and Ricky
6.  Margo and Lamont
7.  Fred and Jack
8.  J. C. and Cora
9.  Marjorie and Throckmorton
10. Pansy and Titus

a.  Secretary
b.  Niece
c.  Traveling companion
d.  Roommates
e.  Brother
f.  Neighbor
g.  Wife
h.  Sister
i.  Husband
j.  Friendly enemies

*Jay Jostlyn* – Mr. District Attorney

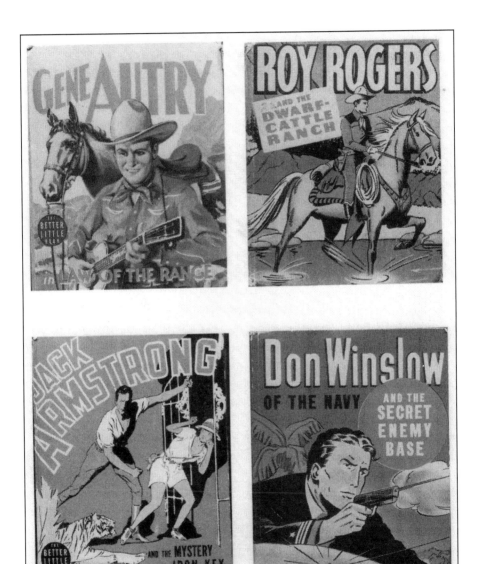

*Big Little Books*

*Sam Hearn – Schlepperman on* The Jack Benny Show

# Quiz #44

## MATCH THE RADIO STAR WITH THE MOVIE
*(Answers on Page 138)*

1. Al Jolson
2. Bob Hope
3. Jack Webb
4. Alan Ladd
5. Eve Arden
6. Jack Benny
7. Jimmy Durante
8. Marie Wilson
9. Eddie Cantor
10. Fred Allen


a. *Shayne*
b. *The Horn Blows at Midnight*
c. *My Friend Irma*
d. *Jumbo*
e. *Beau James*
f. *The Jazz Singer*
g. *Whoopie*
h. *Love Thy Neighbor*
i. *Stage Door*
j. *Pete Kelly's Blues*

*Penny arcade cards*

*Cary Grant on* Suspense

*Tickets to radio shows.*

# ANSWERS

## QUIZ #1 *(from page 5)*

1. Summerfield
2. Water Commissioner
3. Kraft Cheese
4. Walter Tetley
5. He was a druggist.
6. Lillian Randolph
7. Floyd
8. Bullard
9. Bronco
10. The Jolly Boys

## QUIZ #2 *(from page 7)*

1. c
2. e
3. h
4. d
5. i
6. b
7. g
8. a
9. j
10. f

## QUIZ #3    *(from page 9)*
1. Yale
2. *Valiant Lady*
3. "3 Skeleton Key"
4. *The Saint*
5. Simon Templar
6. He was a detective.
7. Art
8. *House of Wax*
9. Mystery Night
10. Mystery

## QUIZ #4    *(from page 13)*
1. b
2. d
3. h
4. g
5. i
6. c
7. j
8. f
9. e
10. a

## QUIZ #5    *(from page 15)*
1. Egg
2. Atlantic
3. Lay's
4. Camay
5. Green Giant
6. Wonder Bread
7. Pep
8. Gorton
9. V-8
10. Bud's

## QUIZ #6 *(from page 19)*

1. Peavey
2. The Great Gildersleeve
3. Little Beaver
4. Smilin' Ed McConnell
5. Kay Kyser
6. Jimmy Durante
7. Jerry Colona
8. Kate Smith
9. Teeny
10. Al Pearce

## QUIZ #7 *(from page 23)*

1. Ozzie Nelson and Harriet Hilliard
2. Red Skelton
3. Nothing
4. Billy May
5. International Silver
6. Emmy Lou
7. Verne Smith
8. Thorny
9. 1847 Rogers Road
10. Ozzie Nelson

## QUIZ #8 *(from page 29)*

1. b
2. d
3. g
4. i
5. h
6. j
7. c
8. a
9. f
10. e

## QUIZ #9    *(from page 33)*

1. *The Horn and Hardart Children's Hour*
2. *Let's Pretend*
3. Seymour Fingerhood
4. Molly's daughter Rosalie
5. Junior
6. *The Henry Morgan Show*
7. Gerard
8. Francis
9. *The Man with the Golden Arm*
10. Top Cat

## QUIZ #10    *(from page 35)*

1. Patty, LaVerne, and Maxine
2. Minneapolis
3. Glenn Miller
4. "Bei Mir Bist Du Shain"
5. "Rum and Coca-Cola"
6. Morey Amsterdam
7. "Beer Barrel Polka"
8. "Apple Blossom Time" and "Don't Sit Under the Apple Tree"
9. Maxine
10. "Over Here"

## QUIZ #11    *(from page 37)*

1. c
2. f
3. i
4. h
5. a
6. g
7. e
8. j
9. d
10. b

## QUIZ #12    *(from page 39)*

1. Sgt. Preston's dog
2. *The Chicago Star*
3. Spike Jones
4. Parkyakarkas
5. Walter Winchell
6. Red Skelton
7. Eddie Anderson
8. Louella Parsons
9. Bed Albright
10. The Hindenburg

## QUIZ #13    *(from page 41)*

1. True
2. False (It was hosted by Jack Barry.)
3. True
4. True
5. False
6. False (He was the quizmaster on *It Pays To Be Ignorant*)
7. True
8. False (The bandleader was Sammy Kaye.)
9. True
10. True

## QUIZ #14    *(from page 42)*

1. Jean Hersholt
2. Paul Whiteman
3. *Leave It To Joan*
4. Johnny Dollar
5. *Bulldog Drummond*
6. Lucky Strike Means Fine Tobacco
7. Philip Morris
8. Don and Jim
9. Harry Frankel
10. Jeff Regan

## QUIZ #15    *(from page 43)*

1. c
2. g
3. h
4. b
5. a
6. f
7. i
8. e
9. j
10. d

## QUIZ #16    *(from page 45)*

1. d
2. g
3. h
4. f
5. c
6. b
7. a
8. j
9. e
10. i

## QUIZ #17    *(from page 47)*

1. Horace
2. Jones
3. Clifton
4. Davidson
5. Pansy
6. Jones
7. Connie
8. Cranston
9. Paul
10. Bumstead

## QUIZ #18    *(from page 49)*

1. Wheaties
2. Duffy's Tavern
3. Denny
4. Dorothy Kilgallen
5. Evelyn
6. Frank Morgan
7. *The Edgar Bergen and Charlie McCarthy Show*
8. Rudy Vallee
9. *Can You Top This?*
10. Luigi Basco

## QUIZ #19    *(from page 51)*

1. True
2. False  (It was *The Whistler.*)
3. False  (It was *Ellery Queen.*)
4. True
5. True
6. False  (It was Mel Allen.)
7. True
8. False  (It was Jack Pearl.)
9. True
10. False

## QUIZ #20    *(from page 53)*

1. Owen Patrick McNulty
2. 1939
3. Kenny Baker
4. Verna Felton
5. *A Day in the Life of Dennis Day*
6. Soda jerk
7. Mildred
8. Johnny Appleseed
9. "Clancy Lowered the Boom"
10. "Mam'selle"

## QUIZ #21    *(from page 55)*

1. b
2. c
3. a
4. c
5. b
6. b
7. a
8. c
9. a
10. c

## QUIZ #22    *(from page 59)*

RADIO:
Judy Canova
Goodman Ace
Vic and Sade
Bob Burns
Lou Lehr

TELEVISION:
Phil Silvers
Joey Bishop
Larry David
Johnny Carson
Jerry Seinfeld

RADIO & TELEVISION:
Bob Hope
Ozzie and Harriet
Red Skelton
Amos 'n' Andy
Garry Moore

# QUIZ #23    *(from page 63)*

1. Billy Mills
2. The Old Timer
3. Gale Gordon
4. Beulah
5. Wallace Wimple
6. Myrt
7. "T'ain't funny, McGee."
8. Writers of the show
9. 9:30 EST
10. "Good night, all."

# QUIZ #24    *(from page 67)*

1. Banjamin Kubelsky
2. Waukegan, Illinois
3. George Burns
4. Frank Parker
5. The Navy (World War I)
6. Frank Nelson
7. Verna Felton
8. Liveey
9. Sheldon Leonard
10. Professor LeBlanc

# QUIZ #25    *(from page 69)*

1. Allen's Alley
2. Pansy
3. Pierre
4. Five
5. *The Linit Bath Club Review*
6. One Long Pan
7. Beauregard
8. Kenny Delmar
9. Herman Wouk
10. "Old Orchard is so boring that the tide once went out and never came back."

# QUIZ #26　*(from page 75)*

1. Crisco
2. Pabst Blue Ribbon
3. Birdseye
4. Chicken of the Sea
5. Blackstone
6. Westinghouse
7. Howard Johnson's
8. White Rain
9. Raid
10. Aqua Velva

# QUIZ #27　*(from page 77)*

1. b
2. a
3. b
4. b
5. c
6. a
7. All three
8. c
9. c
10. a

# QUIZ #28　*(from page 79)*

1. Carton E. Morse
2. *When a Girl Marries*
3. *Backstage Wife*
4. Joyce Jordan
5. Mother and daughter
6. Laurel
7. Young Widder Brown
8. 1925
9. Aunt Jenny
10. She owned a lumberyard.

# QUIZ #29 *(from page 81)*

1. Hop Harrigan
2. *Gangbusters*
3. John Guedel
4. George Seaton
5. Abbot and Costello
6. Lionel Standor
7. *Grand Central Station*
8. Kate Smith
9. *Lights Out*
10. He was a singer.

# QUIZ #30 *(from page 83)*

1. Joe Friday
2. Sergeant
3. Los Angeles Police Department
4. His mother
5. Ben Romero
6. Frank Smith
7. 714
8. He was a big Babe Ruth fan, and Babe had hit 714 home runs.
9. "Just the facts, ma'am."
10. Walter Schuman

# QUIZ #31 *(from page 85)*

1. *Inner Sanctum*
2. *Superman*
3. *Boston Blackie*
4. *Suspense*
5. *Mr. District Attorney*
6. *Lorenzo Jones*
7. *The Lone Ranger*
8. *Ma Perkins*
9. *Bulldog Drummond*
10. *Sam Spade*

## QUIZ #32    *(from page 87)*

1. e
2. g
3. h
4. c
5. b
6. i
7. a
8. j
9. d
10. f

## QUIZ #33    *(from page 91)*

1. *Gene Autry's Melody Ranch*
2. Doublemint Gum
3. Pat Buttram
4. Mr. Autery
5. The Cass County Boys
6. "Back in the Saddle Again"
7. Charlie Lyon
8. "Now, here's the boss-man himself, America's favorite cowboy, Gene Autry."
9. "Rudolph, the Red Nosed Reindeer"
10. The California Angels

## QUIZ #34    *(from page 95)*

1. a
2. b
3. b
4. c
5. b
6. c
7. a
8. a
9. c
10. b

# QUIZ #35   *(from page 97)*

1. e
2. c
3. g
4. i
5. h
6. a
7. j
8. b
9. f
10. d

# QUIZ #36   *(from page 99)*

1. Richard
2. David Rose
3. Junior
4. "I dood it again."
5. A drunk
6. Guzzler's Gin
7. "Holiday For Strings"
8. Cauliflower McPugg
9. The Four Knights
10. "Well, here I am."

# QUIZ #37   *(from page 101)*

1. c
2. f
3. a
4. b
5. g
6. h
7. i
8. j
9. e
10. d

## QUIZ #38  *(from page 103)*

1. Fannie Borach
2. *The Ziegfeld Follies*
3. Eddie Cantor
4. "My Man"
5. Frank White, Nicky Arndtstein, and Billy Rose
6. Seven
7. Sycamore Terrace
8. *Maxwell House Coffee Time*
9. *Funny Girl* and *Funny Lady*
10. Barbra Streisand

## QUIZ #39  *(from page 105)*

1. A monocle
2. Effie Klinker
3. W. C. Fields
4. Ersel Twing
5. "Friends, and you are my friends…"
6. "Mortimer, how can you be so stupid?"
7. "I'll clip ya. So help me, I'll mow ya down."
8. Blanche & John
9. Ray Noble
10. Chase & Sanborn and Coca-Cola

## QUIZ #40  *(from page 111)*

1. Camel
2. Kool
3. Philip Morris
4. Winston
5. Kent
6. L & M
7. Pall Mall
8. Salem, Salem
9. Newport
10. Lucky Strike

## QUIZ #41     *(from page 112)*

1. e
2. d
3. h
4. j
5. f
6. a
7. i
8. b
9. g
10. c

## QUIZ #42     *(from page 113)*

1. d
2. c
3. f
4. g
5. i
6. h
7. e
8. a
9. j
10. b

## QUIZ #43     *(from page 115)*

1. d
2. h
3. a
4. g
5. e
6. c
7. j
8. i
9. b
10. f

## QUIZ #44 *(from page 119)*

1. f
2. e
3. j
4. a
5. i
6. b
7. d
8. c
9. g
10. h

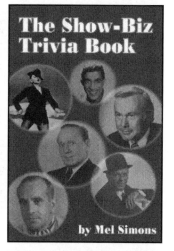
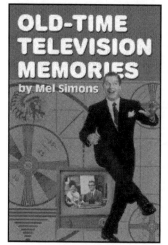

All just $14.95

E-books also
available!

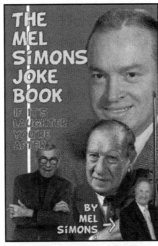

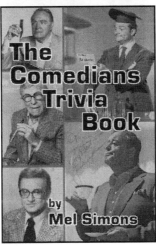
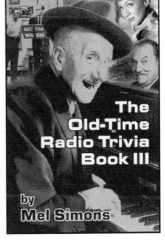

Made in the USA
Middletown, DE
07 July 2016